The Gospel According to
John

VERITAS

The **Gospel** According to

John

(1:1–21:25)

VERITAS
www.veritas.ie

Published 2012 by
Veritas Publications
7–8 Lower Abbey Street
Dublin 1
Ireland
publications@veritas.ie
www.veritas.ie

ISBN 978 1 84730 390 5

10 9 8 7 6 5 4 3 2 1

A catalogue record for this book is available from the British Library.

Designed by Dara O'Connor, Veritas
Printed in Ireland by W&G Baird Ltd, Antrim

Contents

The **Gospel** According to

John

(1:1–21:25)

Saint John the Evangelist · Vladimir Borovikovsky · 1804–1809

Introduction

The Gospel of John is the fourth book of the New Testament. In comparison to the three Synoptic Gospels of Matthew, Mark and Luke, it has less narrative, and no parables, but is a series of long reflections on Jesus as the Divine Son of God. Chapter 21 states that it derives from the testimony of the 'disciple whom Jesus loved'. This unnamed disciple is especially close to Jesus, and early Church tradition identified him as John the Apostle, one of Jesus' twelve apostles. The youngest of the apostles, John wrote his Gospel late in life, around 100 AD.

The Gospel of John follows the historical order of the events of Jesus' life, but its style and focus is thought to be more reflective, profound and spiritual than the other three Gospels. It takes us behind Jesus' ministry, giving us a glimpse of what it means to believe in Jesus as flesh of the eternal and living God, as the source of light and life. Though John's narrative diverges from the Synoptic Gospels, it is a indeed a 'Gospel', a telling of the Good News.

THE PROLOGUE CONTAINING A BRIEF EPITOME OF THE WHOLE GOSPEL IN THE DOCTRINE OF THE INCARNATION OF THE ETERNAL WORD (1:1-18)

chapter ONE

The **Word Became Flesh**

In the beginning was the Word, and the Word was with God, and the Word was God. ²He was in the beginning with God. ³All things came into being through him, and without him not one thing came into being. What has come into being ⁴in him was life, and the life was the light of all people.

⁵The light shines in the darkness, and the darkness did not overcome it. ⁶There was a man sent from God, whose name was John. ⁷He came as a witness to testify to the light, so that all might believe through him. ⁸He himself was not the light, but he came to testify to the light. ⁹The true light, which enlightens everyone, was coming into the world. ¹⁰He was in the world, and the world came into being through him; yet the world did not know him. ¹¹He came to what was his own, and his own people did not accept him. ¹²But to all who received him, who believed in his name, he gave power to become children of God, ¹³who were born, not of blood or of the will of the flesh or of the will of man, but of God. ¹⁴And the Word became flesh and lived among us, and we have seen his glory, the glory as of a father's only son, full of grace and truth.

¹⁵(John testified to him and cried out, 'This was he of whom I said, "He who comes after me ranks ahead of me because he was before me."') ¹⁶From his fullness we have all received, grace upon grace. ¹⁷The law indeed was given through Moses; grace and truth came through Jesus Christ. ¹⁸No one has ever seen God. It is God the only Son, who is close to the Father's heart, who has made him known.

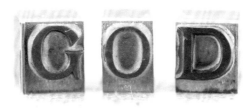

THE FIRST PART RECOUNTING THE PUBLIC LIFE OF JESUS FROM HIS BAPTISM TO THE EVE OF HIS PASSION (1:19–7:52)

The Testimony of John the Baptist

¹⁹This is the testimony given by John when the Jews sent priests and Levites from Jerusalem to ask him, 'Who are you?' ²⁰He confessed and did not deny it, but confessed, 'I am not the Messiah.' ²¹And they asked him, 'What then? Are you Elijah?' He said, 'I am not.' 'Are you the prophet?' He answered, 'No.' ²²Then they said to him, 'Who are you? Let us have an answer for those who sent us. What do you say about yourself?' ²³He said, 'I am the voice of one crying out in the wilderness, "Make straight the way of the Lord,"' as the prophet Isaiah said. ²⁴Now they had been sent from the Pharisees. ²⁵They asked him, 'Why then are you baptising if you are neither the Messiah, nor Elijah, nor the prophet?' ²⁶John answered them, 'I baptise with water. Among you stands one whom you do not know, ²⁷the one who

is coming after me; I am not worthy to untie the thong of his sandal.' ²⁸This took place in Bethany across the Jordan where John was baptising.

The Lamb of God

²⁹The next day he saw Jesus coming toward him and declared, 'Here is the Lamb of God who takes away the sin of the world! ³⁰This is he of whom I said, "After me comes a man who ranks ahead of me because he was before me." ³¹I myself did not know him; but I came baptising with water for

translated means Teacher), 'where are you staying?' [39]He said to them, 'Come and see.' They came and saw where he was staying, and they remained with him that day. It was about four o'clock in the afternoon. [40]One of the two who heard John speak and followed him was Andrew, Simon Peter's brother. [41]He first found his brother Simon and said to him, 'We have found the Messiah' (which is translated Anointed). [42]He brought Simon to Jesus, who looked at him and said, 'You are Simon son of John. You are to be called Cephas' (which is translated Peter).

Jesus Calls Philip and Nathanael

[43]The next day Jesus decided to go to Galilee. He found Philip and said to him, 'Follow me.' [44]Now Philip was from Bethsaida, the city of Andrew and Peter. [45]Philip found Nathanael and said to him, 'We have found him about whom Moses in the law and also the prophets wrote, Jesus son of Joseph from Nazareth.' [46]Nathanael said to him, 'Can anything good come out of Nazareth?' Philip said to him, 'Come and see.' [47]When Jesus saw Nathanael coming toward him, he said of him, 'Here is truly an Israelite in whom there is no deceit!' [48]Nathanael asked him, 'Where did you get to know me?' Jesus answered, 'I saw you under the fig tree before Philip called you.' [49]Nathanael replied, 'Rabbi, you are the Son of God! You are the King of Israel!' [50]Jesus answered, 'Do you believe because I told you that I saw you under the fig tree? You will see greater things than these.' [51]And he said to him, 'Very truly, I tell you, you will see heaven opened and the angels of God ascending and descending upon the Son of Man.'

this reason, that he might be revealed to Israel.' [32]And John testified, 'I saw the Spirit descending from heaven like a dove, and it remained on him. [33]I myself did not know him, but the one who sent me to baptise with water said to me, "He on whom you see the Spirit descend and remain is the one who baptises with the Holy Spirit." [34]And I myself have seen and have testified that this is the Son of God.'

The First Disciples of Jesus

[35]The next day John again was standing with two of his disciples, [36]and as he watched Jesus walk by, he exclaimed, 'Look, here is the Lamb of God!' [37]The two disciples heard him say this, and they followed Jesus. [38]When Jesus turned and saw them following, he said to them, 'What are you looking for?' They said to him, 'Rabbi' (which

'Look, here is the Lamb of God!'

chapter TWO

The **Wedding** at **Cana**

On the third day there was a wedding in Cana of Galilee, and the mother of Jesus was there. ²Jesus and his disciples had also been invited to the wedding. ³When the wine gave out, the mother of Jesus said to him, 'They have no wine.' ⁴And Jesus said to her, 'Woman, what concern is that to you and to me? My hour has not yet come.' ⁵His mother said to the servants, 'Do whatever he tells you.' ⁶Now standing there were six stone water jars for the Jewish rites of purification, each holding twenty or thirty gallons. ⁷Jesus said to them, 'Fill the jars with water.' And they filled them up to the brim. ⁸He said to them, 'Now draw some out, and take it to the chief steward.' So they took it. ⁹When the steward tasted the water that had become wine, and did not know where it came from (though the servants who had drawn the water knew), the steward called the bridegroom ¹⁰and said to him, 'Everyone serves the good wine first, and then the inferior wine after the guests have become drunk. But you have kept the good wine until now.' ¹¹Jesus did this, the first of his signs, in Cana of Galilee, and revealed his glory; and his disciples believed in him. ¹²After this he went down to Capernaum with his mother, his brothers, and his disciples; and they remained there a few days.

Jesus Cleanses the **Temple**

¹³The Passover of the Jews was near, and Jesus went up to Jerusalem. ¹⁴In the temple he found people selling cattle, sheep, and doves, and the money changers seated at their tables. ¹⁵Making a whip of cords, he drove all of them out of the temple, both the sheep and the cattle. He also poured out the coins of the money changers and overturned their tables. ¹⁶He told those who were selling the doves, 'Take these things out of here! Stop making my Father's house a marketplace!' ¹⁷His disciples remembered that it was written, 'Zeal for your house will consume me.' ¹⁸The Jews then said to him, 'What sign can you show us for doing this?' ¹⁹Jesus answered them, 'Destroy this temple, and in three days I will raise it up.' ²⁰The Jews then said, 'This temple has been under construction for forty-six years, and will you raise it up in three days?' ²¹But he was speaking of the temple of his body. ²²After he was raised from the dead, his disciples remembered that he had said this; and they believed the scripture and the word that Jesus had spoken.

²³When he was in Jerusalem during the Passover festival, many believed in his name because they saw the signs that he was doing. ²⁴But Jesus on his part would not entrust himself to them, because he knew all people ²⁵and needed no one to testify about anyone; for he himself knew what was in everyone.

chapter THREE

Nicodemus Visits Jesus

Now there was a Pharisee named Nicodemus, a leader of the Jews. [2]He came to Jesus by night and said to him, 'Rabbi, we know that you are a teacher who has come from God; for no one can do these signs that you do apart from the presence of God.' [3]Jesus answered him, 'Very truly, I tell you, no one can see the kingdom of God without being born from above.' [4]Nicodemus said to him, 'How can anyone be born after having grown old? Can one enter a second time into the mother's womb and be born?' [5]Jesus answered, 'Very truly, I tell you, no one can enter the kingdom of God without being born of water and Spirit. [6]What is born of the flesh is flesh, and what is born of the Spirit is spirit. [7]Do not be astonished that I said to you, "You must be born from above." [8]The wind blows where it chooses, and you hear the sound of it, but you do not know where it comes from or where it goes. So it is with everyone who is born of the Spirit.' [9]Nicodemus said to him, 'How can these things be?' [10]Jesus answered him, 'Are you a teacher of Israel, and yet you do not understand these things? [11]Very truly, I tell you, we speak of what we know and testify to what we have seen; yet you do not receive our testimony. [12]If I have told you about earthly things and you do not believe, how can you believe if I tell you about heavenly things? [13]No one has ascended into heaven except the one who descended from heaven, the Son of Man. [14]And just as Moses lifted up the serpent in the wilderness, so must the Son of Man be lifted up, [15]that whoever believes in him may have eternal life. [16]For God so loved the world that he gave his only Son, so that everyone who believes in him may not perish but may have eternal life. [17]Indeed, God did not send the Son into the world

to condemn the world, but in order that the world might be saved through him. [18]Those who believe in him are not condemned; but those who do not believe are condemned already, because they have not believed in the name of the only Son of God. [19]And this is the judgement, that the light has come into the world, and people loved darkness rather than light because their deeds were evil. [20]For all who do evil hate the light and do not come to the light, so that their deeds may not be exposed. [21]But those who do what is true come to the light, so that it may be clearly seen that their deeds have been done in God.'

Jesus and John the Baptist

[22]After this Jesus and his disciples went into the Judean countryside, and he spent some time

there with them and baptised. [23]John also was baptising at Aenon near Salim because water was abundant there; and people kept coming and were being baptised [24]– John, of course, had not yet been thrown into prison. [25]Now a discussion about purification arose between John's disciples and a Jew. [26]They came to John and said to him, 'Rabbi, the one who was with you across the Jordan, to whom you testified, here he is baptising, and all are going to him.' [27]John answered, 'No one can receive anything except what has been given from heaven. [28]You yourselves are my witnesses that I said, "I am not the Messiah, but I have been sent ahead of him." [29]He who has the bride is the bridegroom. The friend of the bridegroom, who stands and hears him, rejoices greatly at the bridegroom's voice. For this reason my joy has been fulfilled. [30]He must increase, but I must decrease.'

The One Who Comes from Heaven

[31]The one who comes from above is above all; the one who is of the earth belongs to the earth and speaks about earthly things. The one who comes from heaven is above all. [32]He testifies to what he has seen and heard, yet no one accepts his testimony. [33]Whoever has accepted his testimony has certified this, that God is true. [34]He whom God has sent speaks the words of God, for he gives the Spirit without measure. [35]The Father loves the Son and has placed all things in his hands. [36]Whoever believes in the Son has eternal life; whoever disobeys the Son will not see life, but must endure God's wrath.

chapter FOUR

Jesus and the Woman of Samaria

Now when Jesus learned that the Pharisees had heard, 'Jesus is making and baptising more disciples than John' ²– although it was not Jesus himself but his disciples who baptised – ³he left Judea and started back to Galilee.
⁴But he had to go through Samaria. ⁵So he came to a Samaritan city called Sychar, near the plot of ground that Jacob had given to his son Joseph. ⁶Jacob's well was there, and Jesus, tired out by his journey, was sitting by the well. It was about noon. ⁷A Samaritan woman came to draw water, and Jesus said to her, 'Give me a drink.' ⁸(His disciples had gone to the city to buy food.) ⁹The Samaritan woman said to him, 'How is it that you, a Jew, ask a drink of me, a woman of Samaria?' (Jews do not share things in common with Samaritans.) ¹⁰Jesus answered her, 'If you knew the gift of God, and who it is that is saying to you, "Give me a drink," you would have asked him, and he would have given you living water.' ¹¹The woman said to him, 'Sir, you have no bucket, and the well is deep. Where do you get that living water? ¹²Are you greater than our ancestor Jacob, who gave us the well, and with his sons and his flocks drank from it?' ¹³Jesus said to her, 'Everyone who drinks of this water will be thirsty again, ¹⁴but those who drink of the water that I will give them will never be thirsty. The water that I will give will become in them a spring of

water gushing up to eternal life.' [15]The woman said to him, 'Sir, give me this water, so that I may never be thirsty or have to keep coming here to draw water.' [16]Jesus said to her, 'Go, call your husband, and come back.' [17]The woman answered him, 'I have no husband.' Jesus said to her, 'You are right in saying, "I have no husband"; [18]for you have had five husbands, and the one you have now is not your husband. What you have said is true!' [19]The woman said to him, 'Sir, I see that you are a prophet. [20]Our ancestors worshiped on this mountain, but you say that the place where people must worship is in Jerusalem.' [21]Jesus said to her, 'Woman, believe me, the hour is coming when you will worship the Father neither on this mountain nor in Jerusalem. [22]You worship what you do not know; we worship what we know, for salvation is from the Jews. [23]But the hour is coming, and is now here, when the true worshipers will worship the Father in spirit and truth, for the Father seeks such as these to worship him. [24]God is spirit, and those who worship him must worship in spirit and truth.' [25]The woman said to him, 'I know that Messiah is coming' (who is called Christ). 'When he comes, he will proclaim all things to us.' [26]Jesus said to her, 'I am he, the one who is speaking to you.' [27]Just then his disciples came. They were astonished that he was speaking with a woman, but no one said, 'What do you want?' or, 'Why are you speaking with her?' [28]Then the woman left her water jar and went back to the city. She said to the people, [29]'Come and see a man who told me everything I have ever done! He cannot be the Messiah, can he?' [30]They left the city and were on their way to him. [31]Meanwhile the disciples were urging him, 'Rabbi, eat something.' [32]But he said to them, 'I have food to eat that you do not know about.' [33]So the disciples said to one another, 'Surely no one has brought him something to eat?' [34]Jesus said to them, 'My food is to do the will of him who sent

me and to complete his work. [35]Do you not say, "Four months more, then comes the harvest"? But I tell you, look around you, and see how the fields are ripe for harvesting. [36]The reaper is already receiving wages and is gathering fruit for eternal life, so that sower and reaper may rejoice together. [37]For here the saying holds true, "One sows and another reaps." [38]I sent you to reap that for which you did not labour. Others have laboured, and you have entered into their labour.' [39]Many Samaritans from that city believed in him because of the woman's testimony, 'He told me everything I have ever done.' [40]So when the Samaritans came to him, they asked him to stay with them; and he stayed there two days. [41]And many more believed because of his word. [42]They said to the woman, 'It is no longer because of what you said that we believe, for we have heard for ourselves, and we know that this is truly the Saviour of the world.'

Jesus Returns to Galilee

⁴³When the two days were over, he went from that place to Galilee ⁴⁴(for Jesus himself had testified that a prophet has no honour in the prophet's own country). ⁴⁵When he came to Galilee, the Galileans welcomed him, since they had seen all that he had done in Jerusalem at the festival; for they too had gone to the festival.

Jesus Heals an Official's Son

⁴⁶Then he came again to Cana in Galilee where he had changed the water into wine. Now there was a royal official whose son lay ill in Capernaum. ⁴⁷When he heard that Jesus had come from Judea to Galilee, he went and begged him to come down and heal his son, for he was at the point of

death. ⁴⁸Then Jesus said to him, 'Unless you see signs and wonders you will not believe.' ⁴⁹The official said to him, 'Sir, come down before my little boy dies.' ⁵⁰Jesus said to him, 'Go; your son will live.' The man believed the word that Jesus spoke to him and started on his way. ⁵¹As he was going down, his slaves met him and told him that his child was alive. ⁵²So he asked them the hour when he began to recover, and they said to him, 'Yesterday at one in the afternoon the fever left him.' ⁵³The father realised that this was the hour when Jesus had said to him, 'Your son will live.' So he himself believed, along with his whole household. ⁵⁴Now this was the second sign that Jesus did after coming from Judea to Galilee.

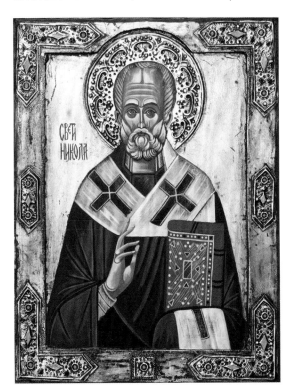

'Unless you see signs and wonders you will not believe.'

while I am making my way, someone else steps down ahead of me.' [8]Jesus said to him, 'Stand up, take your mat and walk.' [9]At once the man was made well, and he took up his mat and began to walk. Now that day was a sabbath. [10]So the Jews said to the man who had been cured, 'It is the sabbath; it is not lawful for you to carry your mat.' [11]But he answered them, 'The man who made me well said to me, "Take up your mat and walk."' [12]They asked him, 'Who is the man who said to you, "Take it up and walk"?' [13]Now the man who had been healed did not know who it was, for Jesus had disappeared in the crowd that was there. [14]Later Jesus found him in the temple and said to him, 'See, you have been made well! Do not sin any more, so that nothing worse happens to you.' [15]The man went away and told the Jews that it was Jesus who had made him well. [16]Therefore the Jews started persecuting Jesus, because he was doing such things on the sabbath. [17]But Jesus answered them, 'My Father is still working, and I also am working.' [18]For this reason the Jews were seeking all the more to kill him, because he was not only breaking the sabbath, but was also calling God his own Father, thereby making himself equal to God.

chapter FIVE

Jesus Heals on the Sabbath

After this there was a festival of the Jews, and Jesus went up to Jerusalem. [2]Now in Jerusalem by the Sheep Gate there is a pool, called in Hebrew Beth-zatha, which has five porticoes. [3]In these lay many invalids – blind, lame, and paralysed. [5]One man was there who had been ill for thirty-eight years. [6]When Jesus saw him lying there and knew that he had been there a long time, he said to him, 'Do you want to be made well?' [7]The sick man answered him, 'Sir, I have no one to put me into the pool when the water is stirred up; and

The **Authority** of the **Son**

¹⁹Jesus said to them, 'Very truly, I tell you, the Son can do nothing on his own, but only what he sees the Father doing; for whatever the Father does, the Son does likewise. ²⁰The Father loves the Son and shows him all that he himself is doing; and he will show him greater works than these, so that you will be astonished. ²¹Indeed, just as the Father raises the dead and gives them life, so also the Son gives life to whomever he wishes. ²²The Father judges no one but has given all judgement to the Son, ²³so that all may honour the Son just as they honour the Father. Anyone who does not honour the Son does not honour the Father who sent him. ²⁴Very truly, I tell you, anyone who hears my word and believes him who sent me has eternal life, and does not come under judgement, but has passed from death to life. ²⁵'Very truly, I tell you, the hour is coming, and is now here, when the dead will hear the voice of the Son of God, and those who hear will live. ²⁶For just as the Father has life in himself, so he has granted the Son also to have life in himself; ²⁷and he has given him authority to execute judgement, because he is the Son of Man. ²⁸Do not be astonished at this; for the hour is coming when all who are in their graves will hear his voice ²⁹and will come out –

those who have done good, to the resurrection of life, and those who have done evil, to the resurrection of condemnation.

Witnesses to Jesus

³⁰'I can do nothing on my own. As I hear, I judge; and my judgement is just, because I seek to do not my own will but the will of him who sent me. ³¹'If I testify about myself, my testimony is not true. ³²There is another who testifies on my behalf, and I know that his testimony to me is true. ³³You sent messengers to John, and he testified to the truth. ³⁴Not that I accept such human testimony, but I say these things so that you may be saved. ³⁵He was a burning and shining lamp, and you were willing to rejoice for a while in his light. ³⁶But I have a testimony greater than John's. The works that the Father has given me to complete, the very works that I am doing, testify on my behalf that the Father has sent me. ³⁷And the Father who sent me has himself testified on my behalf. You have never heard his voice or seen his form, ³⁸and you do not have his word abiding in you, because you do not believe him whom he has sent. ³⁹'You search the scriptures because you think that in them you have eternal life; and it is they that testify on my behalf. ⁴⁰Yet you refuse to come to me to have life. ⁴¹I do not accept glory from human beings. ⁴²But I know that you do not have the love of God in you. ⁴³I have come in my Father's name, and you do not accept me; if another comes in his own name, you will accept him. ⁴⁴How can you believe when you accept glory from one another and do not seek the glory that comes from the one who alone is God? ⁴⁵Do not think that I will accuse you before the Father; your accuser is Moses, on whom you have set your hope. ⁴⁶If you believed Moses, you would believe me, for he wrote about me. ⁴⁷But if you do not believe what he wrote, how will you believe what I say?'

chapter SIX

Feeding the Five Thousand

After this Jesus went to the other side of the Sea of Galilee, also called the Sea of Tiberias. [2]A large crowd kept following him, because they saw the signs that he was doing for the sick. [3]Jesus went up the mountain and sat down there with his disciples. [4]Now the Passover, the festival of the Jews, was near. [5]When he looked up and saw a large crowd coming toward him, Jesus said to Philip, 'Where are we to buy bread for these people to eat?' [6]He said this to test him, for he himself knew what he was going to do. [7]Philip answered him, 'Six months' wages would not buy enough bread for each of them to get a little.' [8]One of his disciples, Andrew, Simon Peter's brother, said to him, [9]'There is a boy here who has five barley loaves and two fish. But what are they among so many people?' [10]Jesus said, 'Make the people sit down.' Now there was a great deal of grass in the place; so they sat down, about five thousand in all. [11]Then Jesus took the loaves, and when he had given thanks, he distributed them to those who were seated; so also the fish, as much as they wanted. [12]When they were satisfied, he told his disciples, 'Gather up the fragments left over, so that nothing may be lost.' [13]So they gathered them up, and from the fragments of the five barley loaves, left by those who had eaten, they filled twelve baskets. [14]When the people saw the sign that he had done, they began to say, 'This is indeed the prophet who is to come into the world.'

[15]When Jesus realised that they were about to come and take him by force to make him king, he withdrew again to the mountain by himself.

Jesus Walks on the Water

[16]When evening came, his disciples went down to the sea, [17]got into a boat, and started across the sea to Capernaum. It was now dark, and Jesus had not yet come to them. [18]The sea became rough because a strong wind was blowing. [19]When they had rowed about three or four miles, they saw Jesus walking on the sea and coming near the boat, and they were terrified. [20]But he said to them, 'It is I; do not be afraid.' [21]Then they wanted to take him into the boat, and immediately the boat reached the land toward which they were going.

The Bread from Heaven

[22]The next day the crowd that had stayed on the other side of the lake saw that there had been only one boat there. They also saw that Jesus had not got into the boat with his disciples, but that his disciples had gone away alone. [23]Then some boats from Tiberias came near the place where they had eaten the bread after the Lord had given thanks. [24]So when the crowd saw that neither Jesus nor his disciples were there, they themselves got into the boats and went to Capernaum looking for Jesus. [25]When they found him on the other side of the sea, they said to him, 'Rabbi, when did you come here?' [26]Jesus answered them, 'Very truly, I tell you, you are looking for me, not because you saw signs, but because you ate your fill of the loaves. [27]Do not work for the food that perishes, but for the food that endures for eternal life, which the Son of Man will give you. For it is on him that God the Father has set his seal.'

²⁸Then they said to him, 'What must we do to perform the works of God?' ²⁹Jesus answered them, 'This is the work of God, that you believe in him whom he has sent.' ³⁰So they said to him, 'What sign are you going to give us then, so that we may see it and believe you? What work are you performing? ³¹Our ancestors ate the manna in the wilderness; as it is written, "He gave them bread from heaven to eat."' ³²Then Jesus said to them, 'Very truly, I tell you, it was not Moses who gave you the bread from heaven, but it is my Father who gives you the true bread from heaven. ³³For the bread of God is that which comes down from heaven and gives life to the world.' ³⁴They said to him, 'Sir, give us this bread always.' ³⁵Jesus said to them, 'I am the bread of life. Whoever comes to me will never be hungry, and whoever believes in me will never be thirsty. ³⁶But I said to you that you have seen me and yet do not believe. ³⁷Everything that the Father gives me will come to me, and anyone who comes to me I will never drive away; ³⁸for I have come down from heaven, not to do my own will, but the will of him who sent me. ³⁹And this is the will of him who sent me, that I should lose nothing of all that he has given me, but raise it up on the last day. ⁴⁰This is indeed the will of my Father, that all who see the Son and believe in him may have eternal life; and I will raise them up on the last day.' ⁴¹Then the Jews began to complain about him because he said, 'I am the bread that came down from heaven.' ⁴²They were saying, 'Is not this Jesus, the son of Joseph, whose father and mother we know? How can he now say, "I have come down from heaven"?' ⁴³Jesus answered them, 'Do not complain among yourselves. ⁴⁴No one can come to me unless drawn by the Father who sent me; and I will raise that person up on the last day. ⁴⁵It is written in the prophets, "And they shall all be taught by God." Everyone who has heard and learned from the Father comes to me. ⁴⁶Not that anyone has seen the Father except the one who is from God; he has seen the Father. ⁴⁷Very truly, I

tell you, whoever believes has eternal life. ⁴⁸I am the bread of life. ⁴⁹Your ancestors ate the manna in the wilderness, and they died. ⁵⁰This is the bread that comes down from heaven, so that one may eat of it and not die. ⁵¹I am the living bread that came down from heaven. Whoever eats of this bread will live forever; and the bread that I will give for the life of the world is my flesh.' ⁵²The Jews then disputed among themselves, saying, 'How can this man give us his flesh to eat?' ⁵³So Jesus said to them, 'Very truly, I tell you, unless you eat the flesh of the Son of Man and drink his blood, you have no life in you. ⁵⁴Those who eat my flesh and drink my blood have eternal life, and I will raise them up on the last day; ⁵⁵for my flesh is true food and my blood is true drink. ⁵⁶Those who eat my flesh and drink my blood abide in me, and I in them. ⁵⁷Just as the living Father sent me, and I live because of the Father, so whoever eats me will live because of me. ⁵⁸This is the bread that came down from heaven, not like that which your ancestors ate, and they died. But the one who eats this bread will live forever.' ⁵⁹He said these things while he was teaching in the synagogue at Capernaum.

The **Words** of Eternal Life

⁶⁰When many of his disciples heard it, they said, 'This teaching is difficult; who can accept it?' ⁶¹But Jesus, being aware that his disciples were complaining about it, said to them, 'Does this offend you? ⁶²Then what if you were to see the Son of Man ascending to where he was before? ⁶³It is the spirit that gives life; the flesh is useless. The words that I have spoken to you are spirit and life. ⁶⁴But among you there are some who do not believe.' For Jesus knew from the first who were the ones that did not believe, and who was the one that would betray him. ⁶⁵And he said, 'For this reason I have told you that no one can come to me unless it is granted by the Father.' ⁶⁶Because of this many of his disciples turned back and no longer went about with him. ⁶⁷So Jesus asked the twelve, 'Do you also wish to go away?' ⁶⁸Simon Peter answered him, 'Lord, to whom can we go? You have the words of eternal life. ⁶⁹We have come to believe and know that you are the Holy One of God.' ⁷⁰Jesus answered them, 'Did I not choose you, the twelve? Yet one of you is a devil.' ⁷¹He was speaking of Judas son of Simon Iscariot, for he, though one of the twelve, was going to betray him.

chapter SEVEN

The Unbelief of Jesus' Brothers

After this Jesus went about in Galilee. He did not wish to go about in Judea because the Jews were looking for an opportunity to kill him. ²Now the Jewish festival of Booths was near. ³So his brothers said to him, 'Leave here and go to Judea so that your disciples also may see the works you are doing; ⁴for no one who wants to be widely known acts in secret. If you do these things, show yourself to the world.' ⁵(For not even his brothers believed in him.) ⁶Jesus said to them, 'My time has not yet come, but your time is always here. ⁷The world cannot hate you, but it hates me because I testify against it that its works are evil. ⁸Go to the festival yourselves. I am not going to this festival, for my time has not yet fully come.' ⁹After saying this, he remained in Galilee.

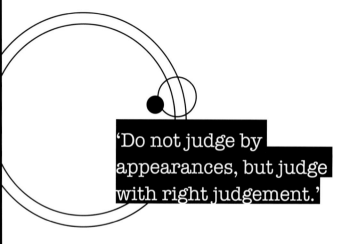

'Do not judge by appearances, but judge with right judgement.'

Jesus at the Festival of Booths

¹⁰But after his brothers had gone to the festival, then he also went, not publicly but as it were in secret. ¹¹The Jews were looking for him at the festival and saying, 'Where is he?' ¹²And there was considerable complaining about him among the crowds. While some were saying, 'He is a good man,' others were saying, 'No, he is deceiving the crowd.' ¹³Yet no one would speak openly about him for fear of the Jews.

¹⁴About the middle of the festival Jesus went up into the temple and began to teach. ¹⁵The Jews were astonished at it, saying, 'How does this man have such learning, when he has never been taught?' ¹⁶Then Jesus answered them, 'My teaching is not mine but his who sent me. ¹⁷Anyone who resolves to do the will of God will know whether the teaching is from God or whether I am speaking on my own. ¹⁸Those who speak on their own seek their own glory; but the one who seeks the glory of him who sent him is true, and there is nothing false in him. ¹⁹'Did not Moses give you the law? Yet none of you keeps the law. Why are you looking for an opportunity to kill me?' ²⁰The crowd answered, 'You have a demon! Who is trying to kill you?' ²¹Jesus answered them, 'I performed one work, and all of you are astonished. ²²Moses gave you circumcision (it is, of course, not from Moses, but from the patriarchs), and you circumcise a man on the sabbath. ²³If a man receives circumcision on the sabbath in order that the law of Moses may not be broken, are you angry with me because I healed a man's whole body on the sabbath? ²⁴Do not judge by appearances, but judge with right judgement.'

'You will search for me, but you will not find me; and where I am, you cannot come.'

Officers Are Sent to Arrest Jesus

³²The Pharisees heard the crowd muttering such things about him, and the chief priests and Pharisees sent temple police to arrest him. ³³Jesus then said, 'I will be with you a little while longer, and then I am going to him who sent me. ³⁴You will search for me, but you will not find me; and where I am, you cannot come.' ³⁵The Jews said to one another, 'Where does this man intend to go that we will not find him? Does he intend to go to the Dispersion among the Greeks and teach the Greeks? ³⁶What does he mean by saying, "You will search for me and you will not find me" and "Where I am, you cannot come"?'

Is This the Christ?

²⁵Now some of the people of Jerusalem were saying, 'Is not this the man whom they are trying to kill? ²⁶And here he is, speaking openly, but they say nothing to him! Can it be that the authorities really know that this is the Messiah? ²⁷Yet we know where this man is from; but when the Messiah comes, no one will know where he is from.' ²⁸Then Jesus cried out as he was teaching in the temple, 'You know me, and you know where I am from. I have not come on my own. But the one who sent me is true, and you do not know him. ²⁹I know him, because I am from him, and he sent me.' ³⁰Then they tried to arrest him, but no one laid hands on him, because his hour had not yet come. ³¹Yet many in the crowd believed in him and were saying, 'When the Messiah comes, will he do more signs than this man has done?'

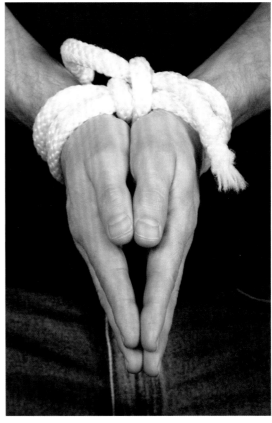

Rivers of Living Water

37On the last day of the festival, the great day, while Jesus was standing there, he cried out, 'Let anyone who is thirsty come to me, 38and let the one who believes in me drink. As the scripture has said, "Out of the believer's heart shall flow rivers of living water."' 39Now he said this about the Spirit, which believers in him were to receive; for as yet there was no Spirit, because Jesus was not yet glorified.

The Unbelief of Those in Authority

Division among the People

40When they heard these words, some in the crowd said, 'This is really the prophet.' 41Others said, 'This is the Messiah.' But some asked, 'Surely the Messiah does not come from Galilee, does he? 42Has not the scripture said that the Messiah is descended from David and comes from Bethlehem, the village where David lived?' 43So there was a division in the crowd because of him. 44Some of them wanted to arrest him, but no one laid hands on him.

45Then the temple police went back to the chief priests and Pharisees, who asked them, 'Why did you not arrest him?' 46The police answered, 'Never has anyone spoken like this!' 47Then the Pharisees replied, 'Surely you have not been deceived too, have you? 48Has any one of the authorities or of the Pharisees believed in him? 49But this crowd, which does not know the law – they are accursed.' 50Nicodemus, who had gone to Jesus before, and who was one of them, asked, 51'Our law does not judge people without first giving them a hearing to find out what they are doing, does it?' 52They replied, 'Surely you are not also from Galilee, are you? Search and you will see that no prophet is to arise from Galilee.'

THE SECOND PART RELATING THE HISTORY OF THE PASSION AND RESURRECTION OF THE SAVIOUR (8:1–21:23)

chapter EIGHT

The **Woman Caught** in **Adultery**

[53]Then each of them went home, while Jesus went to the Mount of Olives. [2]Early in the morning he came again to the temple. All the people came to him and he sat down and began to teach them. [3]The scribes and the Pharisees brought a woman who had been caught in adultery; and making her stand before all of them, [4]they said to him, 'Teacher, this woman was caught in the very act of committing adultery. [5]Now in the law Moses commanded us to stone such women. Now what do you say?' [6]They said this to test him, so that they might have some charge to bring against him. Jesus bent down and wrote with his finger on the ground. [7]When they kept on questioning him, he straightened up and said to them, 'Let anyone among you who is without sin be the first to throw a stone at her.' [8]And once again he bent down and wrote on the ground. [9]When they heard it, they went away, one by one, beginning with the elders; and Jesus was left alone with the woman standing before him. [10]Jesus straightened up and said to her, 'Woman, where are they? Has no one condemned you?' [11]She said, 'No one, sir.' And Jesus said, 'Neither do I condemn you. Go your way, and from now on do not sin again.'

Jesus the **Light** of the **World**

[12]Again Jesus spoke to them, saying, 'I am the light of the world. Whoever follows me will never walk in darkness but will have the light of life.' [13]Then the Pharisees said to him, 'You are testifying on your own behalf; your testimony is not valid.' [14]Jesus answered, 'Even if I testify on my own behalf, my testimony is valid because I know where I have come from and where I am going, but you do not know where I come from or where I am going. [15]You judge by human standards; I judge no one. [16]Yet even if I do judge, my judgement is valid; for it is not I alone who judge, but I and the Father who sent me. [17]In your law it is written that the testimony of two witnesses is valid. [18]I testify on my own behalf, and the Father who sent me testifies on my behalf.' [19]Then they said to him, 'Where is your Father?' Jesus answered, 'You know neither me nor my Father. If you knew me, you would know my Father also.' [20]He spoke these words while he was teaching in the treasury of the temple, but no one arrested him, because his hour had not yet come.

Jesus Foretells His **Death**

[21]Again he said to them, 'I am going away, and you will search for me, but you will die in your sin. Where I am going, you cannot come.' [22]Then the Jews said, 'Is he going to kill himself? Is that what he means by saying, "Where I am going, you cannot come"?' [23]He said to them, 'You are from below, I am from above; you are of this world, I am not of this world. [24]I told you that you would die in your sins, for you will die in your sins unless you believe that I am he.' [25]They said to him, 'Who are you?' Jesus said to them, 'Why do I speak to you at all? [26]I have much to say about you and much to condemn; but the one who sent me is true, and I declare to the world what I have heard from him.' [27]They did not understand that he was speaking to them about the Father. [28]So Jesus said, 'When you have lifted up the Son of Man, then you will realise that I am he, and that I do nothing on my own, but I speak these things as the Father instructed me. [29]And the one who sent me is with me; he has not left me alone, for I always do what is pleasing to him.' [30]As he was saying these things, many believed in him.

True Disciples

[31]Then Jesus said to the Jews who had believed in him, 'If you continue in my word, you are truly my disciples; [32]and you will know the truth, and the truth will make you free.' [33]They answered him, 'We are descendants of Abraham and have never been slaves to anyone. What do you mean by saying, "You will be made free"?' [34]Jesus answered them, 'Very truly, I tell you, everyone who commits sin is a slave to sin. [35]The slave does not have a permanent place in the household; the son has a place there forever. [36]So if the Son makes you free, you will be free indeed. [37]I know that you are descendants of Abraham; yet you look for an opportunity to kill me, because there is no place in you for my word.
[38]I declare what I have seen in the Father's presence; as for you, you should do what you have heard from the Father.'

Jesus and Abraham

[39]They answered him, 'Abraham is our father.' Jesus said to them, 'If you were Abraham's children, you would be doing what Abraham did, [40]but now you are trying to kill me, a man who has told you the truth that I heard from God. This is not what Abraham did. [41]You are indeed doing what your father does.' They said to him, 'We are not illegitimate children; we have one father, God himself.' [42]Jesus said to them, 'If God were your Father, you would love me, for I came from God and now I am here. I did not come on my own, but he sent me. [43]Why do you not understand what I say? It is because you cannot accept my word. [44]You are from your father the devil, and you choose to do your father's desires. He was a murderer from the beginning and does not stand in the truth, because there is no truth in him. When he lies, he speaks according to his own nature, for he is a liar and the father of lies. [45]But because I tell the truth, you do not believe me. [46]Which of you convicts me of sin? If I tell the

truth, why do you not believe me? [47]Whoever is from God hears the words of God. The reason you do not hear them is that you are not from God.' [48]The Jews answered him, 'Are we not right in saying that you are a Samaritan and have a demon?' [49]Jesus answered, 'I do not have a demon; but I honour my Father, and you dishonour me. [50]Yet I do not seek my own glory; there is one who seeks it and he is the judge. [51]Very truly, I tell you, whoever keeps my word will never see death.' [52]The Jews said to him, 'Now we know that you have a demon. Abraham died, and so did the prophets; yet you say, "Whoever keeps my word will never taste death." [53]Are you greater than our father Abraham, who died? The prophets also died. Who do you claim to be?' [54]Jesus answered, 'If I glorify myself, my glory is nothing. It is my Father who glorifies me, he of whom you say, "He is our God," [55]though you do not know him. But I know him; if I would say that I do not know him, I would be a liar like you. But I do know him and I keep his word. [56]Your ancestor Abraham rejoiced that he would see my day; he saw it and was glad.' [57]Then the Jews said to him, 'You are not yet fifty years old, and have you seen Abraham?' [58]Jesus said to them, 'Very truly, I tell you, before Abraham was, I am.' [59]So they picked up stones to throw at him, but Jesus hid himself and went out of the temple.

chapter NINE

A **Man Born Blind** Receives **Sight**

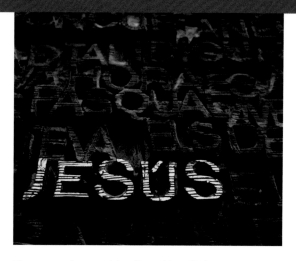

As he walked along, he saw a man blind from birth. ²His disciples asked him, 'Rabbi, who sinned, this man or his parents, that he was born blind?' ³Jesus answered, 'Neither this man nor his parents sinned; he was born blind so that God's works might be revealed in him. ⁴We must work the works of him who sent me while it is day; night is coming when no one can work. ⁵As long as I am in the world, I am the light of the world.' ⁶When he had said this, he spat on the ground and made mud with the saliva and spread the mud on the man's eyes, ⁷saying to him, 'Go, wash in the pool of Siloam' (which means Sent). Then he went and washed and came back able to see. ⁸The neighbours and those who had seen him before as a beggar began to ask, 'Is this not

the man who used to sit and beg?' ⁹Some were saying, 'It is he.' Others were saying, 'No, but it is someone like him.' He kept saying, 'I am the man.' ¹⁰But they kept asking him, 'Then how were your eyes opened?' ¹¹He answered, 'The man called Jesus made mud, spread it on my eyes, and said to me, "Go to Siloam and wash." Then I went and washed and received my sight.' ¹²They said to him, 'Where is he?' He said, 'I do not know.'

The **Pharisees** **Investigate** the **Healing**

¹³They brought to the Pharisees the man who had formerly been blind. ¹⁴Now it was a sabbath day when Jesus made the mud and opened his eyes. ¹⁵Then the Pharisees also began to ask him how he had received his sight. He said to them, 'He put mud on my eyes. Then I washed, and now I see.' ¹⁶Some of the Pharisees said, 'This man is not from God, for he does not observe the sabbath.' But others said, 'How can a man who is a sinner perform such signs?' And they were divided. ¹⁷So they said again to the blind man, 'What do you say about him? It was your eyes he opened.' He said, 'He is a prophet.' ¹⁸The Jews did not believe that he had been blind and had received his sight until they called the parents of the man who had received his sight ¹⁹and asked them, 'Is this your son, who you say was born blind? How then does he now see?' ²⁰His parents answered, 'We know that this is our son, and that he was born blind; ²¹but we do not know how it is that now

he sees, nor do we know who opened his eyes. Ask him; he is of age. He will speak for himself.' [22]His parents said this because they were afraid of the Jews; for the Jews had already agreed that anyone who confessed Jesus to be the Messiah would be put out of the synagogue. [23]Therefore his parents said, 'He is of age; ask him.' [24]So for the second time they called the man who had been blind, and they said to him, 'Give glory to God! We know that this man is a sinner.' [25]He answered, 'I do not know whether he is a sinner. One thing I do know, that though I was blind, now I see.' [26]They said to him, 'What did he do to you? How did he open your eyes?' [27]He answered them, 'I have told you already, and you would not listen. Why do you want to hear it again? Do you also want to become his disciples?' [28]Then they reviled him, saying, 'You are his disciple, but we are disciples of Moses. [29]We know that God has spoken to Moses, but as for this man, we do not know where he comes from.' [30]The man answered, 'Here is an astonishing thing! You do not know where he comes from, and yet he opened my eyes. [31]We know that God does not listen to sinners, but he does listen to one who worships him and obeys his will. [32]Never since the world began has it been heard that anyone opened the eyes of a person born blind. [33]If this man were not from God, he could do nothing.' [34]They answered him, 'You were born entirely in sins, and are you trying to teach us?' And they drove him out.

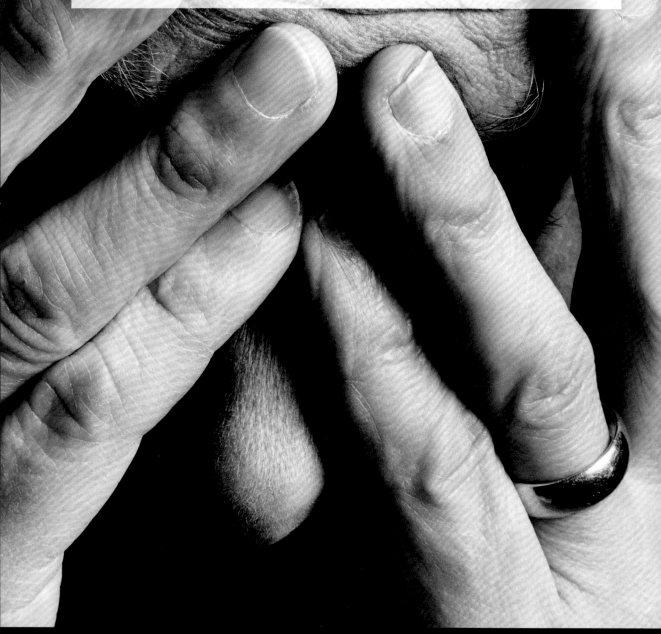

Spiritual Blindness

[35]Jesus heard that they had driven him out, and when he found him, he said, 'Do you believe in the Son of Man?' [36]He answered, 'And who is he, sir? Tell me, so that I may believe in him.' [37]Jesus said to him, 'You have seen him, and the one speaking with you is he.' [38]He said, 'Lord, I believe.' And he worshiped him.

[39]Jesus said, 'I came into this world for judgement so that those who do not see may see, and those who do see may become blind.' [40]Some of the Pharisees near him heard this and said to him, 'Surely we are not blind, are we?' [41]Jesus said to them, 'If you were blind, you would not have sin. But now that you say, "We see," your sin remains.

chapter TEN

Jesus the Good Shepherd

'Very truly, I tell you, anyone who does not enter the sheepfold by the gate but climbs in by another way is a thief and a bandit. ²The one who enters by the gate is the shepherd of the sheep. ³The gatekeeper opens the gate for him, and the sheep hear his voice. He calls his own sheep by name and leads them out. ⁴When he has brought out all his own, he goes ahead of them, and the sheep follow him because they know his voice. ⁵They will not follow a stranger, but they will run from him because they do not know the voice of strangers.' ⁶Jesus used this figure of speech with them, but they did not understand what he was saying to them. ⁷So again Jesus said to them, 'Very truly, I tell you, I am the gate for the sheep. ⁸All who came before me are thieves and bandits; but the sheep did not listen to them. ⁹I am the gate. Whoever enters by me will be saved, and will come in and go out and find pasture. ¹⁰The thief comes only to steal and kill and destroy. I came that they may have life, and have it abundantly. ¹¹'I am the good shepherd. The good shepherd lays down his life for the sheep. ¹²The hired hand, who is not the shepherd and does not own the sheep, sees the wolf coming and leaves the sheep and runs away – and the wolf snatches them and scatters them. ¹³The hired hand runs away because a hired hand does not care for the sheep. ¹⁴I am the good shepherd. I know my own and my own know me, ¹⁵just as the Father knows me and I know the Father. And I lay down my life for the sheep. ¹⁶I have other sheep that do not belong to this fold. I must bring them also, and they will listen to my voice. So there will be one flock, one shepherd. ¹⁷For this reason the Father loves me, because I lay down my life in order to take it up again. ¹⁸No one takes it from me, but I lay it down of my own accord. I have power to lay it down, and I have power to take it up again. I have received this command from my Father.' ¹⁹Again the Jews were divided because of these words. ²⁰Many of them were saying, 'He has a demon and is out of his mind. Why listen to him?' ²¹Others were saying, 'These are not the words of one who has a demon. Can a demon open the eyes of the blind?'

Jesus Is Rejected by the Jews

²²At that time the festival of the Dedication took place in Jerusalem. It was winter, ²³and Jesus was walking in the temple, in the portico of Solomon. ²⁴So the Jews gathered around him and said to him, 'How long will you keep us in suspense? If you are the Messiah, tell us plainly.' ²⁵Jesus answered, 'I have told you, and you do not believe. The works that I do in my Father's name testify to me; ²⁶but you do not believe, because you do not belong to my sheep. ²⁷My sheep hear my voice. I know them, and they follow me. ²⁸I give them eternal life, and they will never perish. No one will snatch them out of my hand. ²⁹What my Father has given me is greater than all else, and no one can snatch it out of the Father's hand. ³⁰The Father and I are one.' ³¹The Jews took up stones again to stone him. ³²Jesus replied, 'I have shown you many good works from the Father. For which of these are you going to stone me?' ³³The Jews answered, 'It is not for a good work that we are going to stone you, but for blasphemy, because you, though only a human being, are making yourself God.' ³⁴Jesus answered, 'Is it not written in your law, "I said, you are gods"? ³⁵If those to whom the word of God came were called 'gods' – and the scripture cannot be annulled – ³⁶can you say that the one whom the Father has sanctified and sent into the world is blaspheming because I said, "I am God's Son"? ³⁷If I am not doing the works of my Father, then do not believe me. ³⁸But if I do them, even though you do not believe me, believe the works, so that you may know and understand that the Father is in me and I am in the Father.'

³⁹Then they tried to arrest him again, but he escaped from their hands. ⁴⁰He went away again across the Jordan to the place where John had been baptising earlier, and he remained there. ⁴¹Many came to him, and they were saying, 'John performed no sign, but everything that John said about this man was true.' ⁴²And many believed in him there.

chapter ELEVEN

The Death of Lazarus

Now a certain man was ill, Lazarus of Bethany, the village of Mary and her sister Martha. ²Mary was the one who anointed the Lord with perfume and wiped his feet with her hair; her brother Lazarus was ill. ³So the sisters sent a message to Jesus, 'Lord, he whom you love is ill.' ⁴But when Jesus heard it, he said, 'This illness does not lead to death; rather it is for God's glory, so that the Son of God may be glorified through it.' ⁵Accordingly, though Jesus loved Martha and her sister and Lazarus, ⁶after having heard that Lazarus was ill, he stayed two days longer in the place where he was. ⁷Then after this he said to the disciples, 'Let us go to Judea again.' ⁸The disciples said to him, 'Rabbi, the Jews were just now trying to stone you, and are you going there again?' ⁹Jesus answered, 'Are there not twelve hours of daylight? Those who walk during the day do not stumble, because they see the light of this world. ¹⁰But those who walk at night stumble, because the light is not in them.' ¹¹After saying this, he told them, 'Our friend Lazarus has fallen asleep, but I am going there to awaken him.' ¹²The disciples said to him, 'Lord, if he has fallen asleep, he will be all right.' ¹³Jesus, however, had been speaking about his death, but they thought that he was referring merely to sleep. ¹⁴Then Jesus told them plainly, 'Lazarus is dead. ¹⁵For your sake I am glad I was not there, so that you may believe. But let us go to him.' ¹⁶Thomas, who was called the Twin, said to his fellow disciples, 'Let us also go, that we may die with him.'

Jesus the Resurrection and the Life

[17]When Jesus arrived, he found that Lazarus had already been in the tomb four days. [18]Now Bethany was near Jerusalem, some two miles away, [19]and many of the Jews had come to Martha and Mary to console them about their brother. [20]When Martha heard that Jesus was coming, she went and met him, while Mary stayed at home. [21]Martha said to Jesus, 'Lord, if you had been here, my brother would not have died. [22]But even now I know that God will give you whatever you ask of him.' [23]Jesus said to her, 'Your brother will rise again.' [24]Martha said to him, 'I know that he will rise again in the resurrection on the last day.' [25]Jesus said to her, 'I am the resurrection and the life. Those who believe in me, even though they die, will live, [26]and everyone who lives and believes in me will never die. Do you believe this?' [27]She said to him, 'Yes, Lord, I believe that you are the Messiah, the Son of God, the one coming into the world.'

Jesus Weeps

[28]When she had said this, she went back and called her sister Mary, and told her privately, 'The Teacher is here and is calling for you.' [29]And when she heard it, she got up quickly and went to him. [30]Now Jesus had not yet come to the village, but was still at the place where Martha had met him. [31]The Jews who were with her in the house, consoling her, saw Mary get up quickly and go out. They followed her because they thought that she was going to the tomb to weep there. [32]When Mary came where Jesus was and saw him, she knelt at his feet and said to him, 'Lord, if you had been here, my brother would not have died.' [33]When Jesus saw her weeping, and the Jews who came with her also weeping, he was greatly disturbed in spirit and deeply moved. [34]He said, 'Where have you laid him?' They said to him, 'Lord, come and see.' [35]Jesus began to weep. [36]So the Jews said, 'See how he loved him!' [37]But some of them said, 'Could not he who opened the eyes of the blind man have kept this man from dying?'

Jesus Raises Lazarus to Life

[38]Then Jesus, again greatly disturbed, came to the tomb. It was a cave, and a stone was lying against it. [39]Jesus said, 'Take away the stone.' Martha, the sister of the dead man, said to him, 'Lord, already there is a stench because he has been dead four days.' [40]Jesus said to her, 'Did I not tell you that if you believed, you would see the glory of God?' [41]So they took away the stone. And Jesus looked upward and said, 'Father, I thank you for having heard me. [42]I knew that you always hear me, but I have said this for the sake of the crowd standing here, so that they may believe that you sent me.' [43]When he had said this, he cried with a loud voice, 'Lazarus, come out!' [44]The dead man came

out, his hands and feet bound with strips of cloth, and his face wrapped in a cloth. Jesus said to them, 'Unbind him, and let him go.'

The Plot to Kill Jesus

45Many of the Jews therefore, who had come with Mary and had seen what Jesus did, believed in him. 46But some of them went to the Pharisees and told them what he had done. 47So the chief priests and the Pharisees called a meeting of the council, and said, 'What are we to do? This man is performing many signs. 48If we let him go on like this, everyone will believe in him, and the Romans will come and destroy both our holy place and our nation.' 49But one of them, Caiaphas, who was high priest that year, said to them, 'You know nothing at all! 50You do not understand that it is better for you to have one man die for the people than to have the whole nation destroyed.' 51He did not say this on his own, but being high priest that year he prophesied that Jesus was about to die for the nation, 52and not for the nation only, but to gather into one the dispersed children of God. 53So from that day on they planned to put him to death. 54Jesus therefore no longer walked about openly among the Jews, but went from there to a town called Ephraim in the region near the wilderness; and he remained there with the disciples. 55Now the Passover of the Jews was near, and many went up from the country to Jerusalem before the Passover to purify themselves. 56They were looking for Jesus and were asking one another as they stood in the temple, 'What do you think? Surely he will not come to the festival, will he?' 57Now the chief priests and the Pharisees had given orders that anyone who knew where Jesus was should let them know, so that they might arrest him.

chapter TWELVE

Mary Anoints Jesus

Six days before the Passover Jesus came to Bethany, the home of Lazarus, whom he had raised from the dead. [2]There they gave a dinner for him. Martha served, and Lazarus was one of those at the table with him. [3]Mary took a pound of costly perfume made of pure nard, anointed Jesus' feet, and wiped them with her hair. The house was filled with the fragrance of the perfume. [4]But Judas Iscariot, one of his disciples (the one who was about to betray him), said, [5]'Why was this perfume not sold for three hundred denarii and the money given to the poor?' [6](He said this not because he cared about the poor, but because he was a thief; he kept the common purse and used to steal what was put into it.) [7]Jesus said, 'Leave her alone. She bought it so that she might keep it for the day of my burial. [8]You always have the poor with you, but you do not always have me.'

The Plot to Kill Lazarus

[9]When the great crowd of the Jews learned that he was there, they came not only because of Jesus but also to see Lazarus, whom he had raised from the dead. [10]So the chief priests planned to put Lazarus to death as well, [11]since it was on account of him that many of the Jews were deserting and were believing in Jesus.

Jesus' Triumphal Entry into Jerusalem

[12]The next day the great crowd that had come to the festival heard that Jesus was coming to Jerusalem. [13]So they took branches of palm trees and went out to meet him, shouting, 'Hosanna! Blessed is the one who comes in the name of the Lord – the King of Israel!' [14]Jesus found a young donkey and sat on it; as it is written: [15] 'Do not be afraid, daughter of Zion. Look, your king is coming, sitting on a donkey's colt!' [16]His disciples did not understand these things at first; but when Jesus was glorified, then they remembered that these things had been written of him and had been done to him. [17]So the crowd that had been with him when he called Lazarus out of the tomb and raised him from the dead continued to testify. [18]It was also because they heard that he had performed this sign that the crowd went to meet him. [19]The Pharisees then said to one another, 'You see, you can do nothing. Look, the world has gone after him!'

Jesus Speaks about His Death

[27]'Now my soul is troubled. And what should I say – "Father, save me from this hour"? No, it is for this reason that I have come to this hour. [28]Father, glorify your name.' Then a voice came from heaven, 'I have glorified it, and I will glorify it again.' [29]The crowd standing there heard it and said that it was thunder. Others said, 'An angel has spoken to him.' [30]Jesus answered, 'This voice has come for your sake, not for mine. [31]Now is the judgement of this world; now the ruler of this world will be driven out. [32]And I, when I am lifted up from the earth, will draw all people to myself.' [33]He said this to indicate the kind of death he was to die. [34]The crowd answered him, 'We have heard from the law that the Messiah remains forever. How can you say that the Son of Man must be lifted up? Who is this Son of Man?' [35]Jesus said to them, 'The light is with you for a little longer. Walk while you have the light, so that the darkness may not overtake you. If you walk in the darkness, you do not know where you are going. [36]While you have the light, believe in the light, so that you may become children of light.'

Some Greeks Wish to See Jesus

[20]Now among those who went up to worship at the festival were some Greeks. [21]They came to Philip, who was from Bethsaida in Galilee, and said to him, 'Sir, we wish to see Jesus.' [22]Philip went and told Andrew; then Andrew and Philip went and told Jesus. [23]Jesus answered them, 'The hour has come for the Son of Man to be glorified. [24]Very truly, I tell you, unless a grain of wheat falls into the earth and dies, it remains just a single grain; but if it dies, it bears much fruit. [25]Those who love their life lose it, and those who hate their life in this world will keep it for eternal life. [26]Whoever serves me must follow me, and where I am, there will my servant be also. Whoever serves me, the Father will honour.

The **Unbelief** of the **People**

After Jesus had said this, he departed and hid from them.

³⁷Although he had performed so many signs in their presence, they did not believe in him. ³⁸This was to fulfil the word spoken by the prophet Isaiah: 'Lord, who has believed our message, and to whom has the arm of the Lord been revealed?' ³⁹And so they could not believe, because Isaiah also said, ⁴⁰'He has blinded their eyes and hardened their heart, so that they might not look with their eyes, and understand with their heart and turn – and I would heal them.' ⁴¹Isaiah said this because he saw his glory and spoke about him. ⁴²Nevertheless many, even of the authorities, believed in him. But because of the Pharisees they did not confess it, for fear that they would be put out of the synagogue; ⁴³for they loved human glory more than the glory that comes from God.

Summary of **Jesus' Teaching**

⁴⁴Then Jesus cried aloud: 'Whoever believes in me believes not in me but in him who sent me. ⁴⁵And whoever sees me sees him who sent me. ⁴⁶I have come as light into the world, so that everyone who believes in me should not remain in the darkness. ⁴⁷I do not judge anyone who hears my words and does not keep them, for I came not to judge the world, but to save the world. ⁴⁸The one who rejects me and does not receive my word has a judge; on the last day the word that I have spoken will serve as judge, ⁴⁹for I have not spoken on my own, but the Father who sent me has himself given me a commandment about what to say and what to speak. ⁵⁰And I know that his commandment is eternal life. What I speak, therefore, I speak just as the Father has told me.'

chapter THIRTEEN

Jesus Washes the Disciples' Feet

Now before the festival of the Passover, Jesus knew that his hour had come to depart from this world and go to the Father. Having loved his own who were in the world, he loved them to the end. [2]The devil had already put it into the heart of Judas son of Simon Iscariot to betray him. And during supper [3]Jesus, knowing that the Father had given all things into his hands, and that he had come from God and was going to God, [4]got up from the table, took off his outer robe, and tied a towel around himself. [5]Then he poured water into a basin and began to wash the disciples' feet and to wipe them with the towel that was tied around him. [6]He came to Simon Peter, who said to him, 'Lord, are you going to wash my feet?' [7]Jesus answered, 'You do not know now what I am doing, but later you will understand.' [8]Peter said to him, 'You will never wash my feet.' Jesus answered, 'Unless I wash you, you have no share with me.' [9]Simon Peter said to him, 'Lord, not my feet only but also my hands and my head!' [10]Jesus said to him, 'One who has bathed does not need to wash, except for the feet, but is entirely clean. And you are clean, though not all of you.' [11]For he knew who was to betray him; for this reason he said, 'Not all of you are clean.' [12]After he had washed their feet, had put on his robe, and had returned to the table, he said to them, 'Do you know what I have done to you? [13]You call me Teacher and Lord – and you are right, for that is what I am. [14]So if I, your Lord and Teacher, have washed your feet, you also ought to wash one

another's feet. [15]For I have set you an example, that you also should do as I have done to you. [16]Very truly, I tell you, servants are not greater than their master, nor are messengers greater than the one who sent them. [17]If you know these things, you are blessed if you do them.

[18]I am not speaking of all of you; I know whom I have chosen. But it is to fulfil the scripture, "The one who ate my bread has lifted his heel against me." [19]I tell you this now, before it occurs, so that when it does occur, you may believe that I am he. [20]Very truly, I tell you, whoever receives one whom I send receives me; and whoever receives me receives him who sent me.'

Jesus Foretells His Betrayal

[21]After saying this Jesus was troubled in spirit, and declared, 'Very truly, I tell you, one of you will betray me.' [22]The disciples looked at one another, uncertain of whom he was speaking. [23]One of his disciples – the one whom Jesus loved – was reclining next to him; [24]Simon Peter therefore motioned to him to ask Jesus of whom he was speaking. [25]So while reclining next to Jesus, he asked him, 'Lord, who is it?' [26]Jesus answered, 'It is the one to whom I give this piece of bread when I have dipped it in the dish.' So when he had dipped the piece of bread, he gave it to Judas son of Simon Iscariot. [27]After he received the piece of bread, Satan entered into him. Jesus said to him, 'Do quickly what you are going to do.' [28]Now no one at the table knew why he said this to him. [29]Some thought that, because Judas had the common purse, Jesus was telling him, 'Buy what we need for the festival'; or, that he should give something to the poor. [30]So, after receiving the piece of bread, he immediately went out. And it was night.

The New Commandment

[31]When he had gone out, Jesus said, 'Now the Son of Man has been glorified, and God has been glorified in him. [32]If God has been glorified in him, God will also glorify him in himself and will glorify him at once. [33]Little children, I am with you only a little longer. You will look for me; and as I said to the Jews so now I say to you, "Where I am going, you cannot come." [34]I give you a new commandment, that you love one another. Just as I have loved you, you also should love one another. [35]By this everyone will know that you are my disciples, if you have love for one another.'

Jesus Foretells Peter's Denial

[36]Simon Peter said to him, 'Lord, where are you going?' Jesus answered, 'Where I am going, you cannot follow me now; but you will follow afterward.' [37]Peter said to him, 'Lord, why can I not follow you now? I will lay down my life for you.' [38]Jesus answered, 'Will you lay down your life for me? Very truly, I tell you, before the cock crows, you will have denied me three times.

chapter FOURTEEN

Jesus the Way to the Father

'Do not let your hearts be troubled. Believe in God, believe also in me. ²In my Father's house there are many dwelling places. If it were not so, would I have told you that I go to prepare a place for you? ³And if I go and prepare a place for you, I will come again and will take you to myself, so that where I am, there you may be also. ⁴And you know the way to the place where I am going.' ⁵Thomas said to him, 'Lord, we do not know where you are going. How can we know the way?' ⁶Jesus said to him, 'I am the way, and the truth, and the life. No one comes to the Father except through me. ⁷If you know me, you will know my Father also. From now on you do know him and have seen him.' ⁸Philip said to him, 'Lord, show us the Father, and we will be satisfied.' ⁹Jesus said to him, 'Have I been with you all this time, Philip, and you still do not know me? Whoever has seen me has seen the Father. How can you say, "Show us the Father"? ¹⁰Do you not believe that I am in the Father and the Father is in me? The words that I say to you I do not speak on my own; but the Father who dwells in me does his works. ¹¹Believe me that I am in the Father and the Father is in me; but if you do not, then believe me because of the works themselves.

¹²Very truly, I tell you, the one who believes in me will also do the works that I do and, in fact, will do greater works than these, because I am going to the Father. ¹³I will do whatever you ask in my name, so that the Father may be glorified in the Son. ¹⁴If in my name you ask me for anything, I will do it.

The **Promise** of the **Holy Spirit**

15'If you love me, you will keep my commandments. 16And I will ask the Father, and he will give you another Advocate, to be with you forever. 17This is the Spirit of truth, whom the world cannot receive, because it neither sees him nor knows him. You know him, because he abides with you, and he will be in you.

18'I will not leave you orphaned; I am coming to you. 19In a little while the world will no longer see me, but you will see me; because I live, you also will live. 20On that day you will know that I am in my Father, and you in me, and I in you. 21They who have my commandments and keep them are those who love me; and those who love me will be loved by my Father, and I will love them and reveal myself to them.' 22Judas (not Iscariot) said to him, 'Lord, how is it that you will reveal yourself to us, and not to the world?' 23Jesus answered him, 'Those who love me will keep my word, and my Father will love them, and we will come to them and make our home with them.

24Whoever does not love me does not keep my words; and the word that you hear is not mine, but is from the Father who sent me.

25'I have said these things to you while I am still with you. 26But the Advocate, the Holy Spirit, whom the Father will send in my name, will teach you everything, and remind you of all that I have said to you. 27Peace I leave with you; my peace I give to you. I do not give to you as the world gives. Do not let your hearts be troubled, and do not let them be afraid.

28You heard me say to you, "I am going away, and I am coming to you." If you loved me, you would rejoice that I am going to the Father, because the Father is greater than I. 29And now I have told you this before it occurs, so that when it does occur, you may believe. 30I will no longer talk much with you, for the ruler of this world is coming. He has no power over me; 31but I do as the Father has commanded me, so that the world may know that I love the Father. Rise, let us be on our way.

chapter FIFTEEN

Jesus the True Vine

'I am the true vine, and my Father is the vinegrower. ²He removes every branch in me that bears no fruit. Every branch that bears fruit he prunes to make it bear more fruit. ³You have already been cleansed by the word that I have spoken to you. ⁴Abide in me as I abide in you. Just as the branch cannot bear fruit by itself unless it abides in the vine, neither can you unless you abide in me. ⁵I am the vine, you are the branches. Those who abide in me and I in them bear much fruit, because apart from me you can do nothing. ⁶Whoever does not abide in me is thrown away like a branch and withers; such branches are gathered, thrown into the fire, and burned. ⁷If you abide in me, and my words abide in you, ask for whatever you wish, and it will be done for you. ⁸My Father is glorified by this, that you bear much fruit and become my disciples.

⁹As the Father has loved me, so I have loved you; abide in my love. ¹⁰If you keep my commandments, you will abide in my love, just as I have kept my Father's commandments and abide in his love. ¹¹I have said these things to you so that my joy may be in you, and that your joy may be complete. ¹²'This is my commandment, that you love one another as I have loved you. ¹³No one has greater love than this, to lay down one's life for one's friends. ¹⁴You are my friends if you do what I command you. ¹⁵I do not call you servants any longer, because the servant does not know what the master is doing; but I have called you friends, because I have made known to you everything that I have heard from my Father. ¹⁶You did not choose me but I chose you. And I appointed you to go and bear fruit, fruit that will last, so that the Father will give you whatever you ask him in my name. ¹⁷I am giving you these commands so that you may love one another.

The World's Hatred

¹⁸'If the world hates you, be aware that it hated me before it hated you. ¹⁹If you belonged to the world, the world would love you as its own. Because you do not belong to the world, but I have chosen you out of the world – therefore the world hates you. ²⁰Remember the word that I said to you, "Servants are not greater than their master." If they persecuted me, they will persecute you; if they kept my word, they will keep yours also. ²¹But they will do all these things to you on account of my name, because they do not know him who sent me. ²²If I had not come and spoken to them, they would not have sin; but now they have no excuse for their sin. ²³Whoever hates me hates my Father also. ²⁴If I had not done among them the works that no one else did, they would not have sin. But now they have seen and hated both me and my Father. ²⁵It was to fulfil the word that is written in their law, "They hated me without a cause."

²⁶'When the Advocate comes, whom I will send to you from the Father, the Spirit of truth who comes from the Father, he will testify on my behalf. ²⁷You also are to testify because you have been with me from the beginning.

chapter SIXTEEN

'I have said these things to you to keep you from stumbling. [2]They will put you out of the synagogues. Indeed, an hour is coming when those who kill you will think that by doing so they are offering worship to God. [3]And they will do this because they have not known the Father or me. [4]But I have said these things to you so that when their hour comes you may remember that I told you about them.

The Work of the Spirit

'I did not say these things to you from the beginning, because I was with you. [5]But now I am going to him who sent me; yet none of you asks me, "Where are you going?" [6]But because I have said these things to you, sorrow has filled your hearts. [7]Nevertheless I tell you the truth: it is to your advantage that I go away, for if I do not go away, the Advocate will not come to you; but if I go, I will send him to you. [8]And when he comes, he will prove the world wrong about sin and righteousness and judgement: [9]about sin, because they do not believe in me; [10]about righteousness, because I am going to the Father and you will see me no longer; [11]about judgement, because the ruler of this world has been condemned. [12]I still have many things to say to you, but you cannot bear them now. [13]When the Spirit of truth comes, he will guide you into all the truth; for he will not speak on his own, but will speak whatever he hears, and he will declare to you the things that are to come. [14]He will glorify me, because he will take what is mine and declare it to you. [15]All that the Father has is mine. For this reason I said that he will take what is mine and declare it to you.

Sorrow Will Turn into Joy

[16]'A little while, and you will no longer see me, and again a little while, and you will see me.' [17]Then some of his disciples said to one another, 'What does he mean by saying to us, "A little while, and you will no longer see me, and again a little while, and you will see me"; and "Because I am going to the Father"?' [18]They said, 'What does he mean by this "a little while"? We do not know what he is talking about.' [19]Jesus knew that they wanted to ask him, so he said to them, 'Are you discussing among yourselves what I meant when I said, "A little while, and you will no longer see me, and again a little while, and you will see me"? [20]Very truly, I tell you, you will weep and mourn, but the world will rejoice; you will have pain, but your pain will turn into joy. [21]When a woman is in labour, she has pain, because her hour has come. But when her child is born, she no longer remembers the anguish because of the joy of having brought a human being into the world. [22]So you have pain now; but I will see you again, and your hearts will rejoice, and no one will take your joy from you.

[23]On that day you will ask nothing of me. Very truly, I tell you, if you ask anything of the Father in my name, he will give it to you. [24]Until now you have not asked for anything in my name. Ask and you will receive, so that your joy may be complete.

Peace for the Disciples

[25]'I have said these things to you in figures of speech. The hour is coming when I will no longer speak to you in figures, but will tell you plainly of the Father. [26]On that day you will ask in my

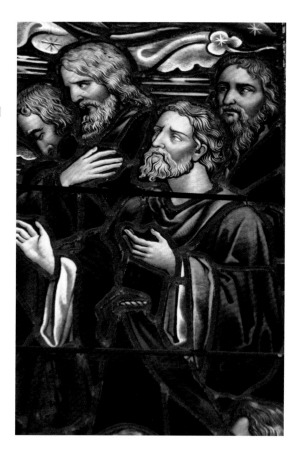

name. I do not say to you that I will ask the Father on your behalf; [27]for the Father himself loves you, because you have loved me and have believed that I came from God.

[28]I came from the Father and have come into the world; again, I am leaving the world and am going to the Father.' [29]His disciples said, 'Yes, now you are speaking plainly, not in any figure of speech! [30]Now we know that you know all things, and do not need to have anyone question you; by this we believe that you came from God.' [31]Jesus answered them, 'Do you now believe? [32]The hour is coming, indeed it has come, when you will be scattered, each one to his home, and you will leave me alone. Yet I am not alone because the Father is with me. [33]I have said this to you, so that in me you may have peace. In the world you face persecution. But take courage; I have conquered the world!'

chapter SEVENTEEN

Jesus Prays for His Disciples

After Jesus had spoken these words, he looked up to heaven and said, 'Father, the hour has come; glorify your Son so that the Son may glorify you, ²since you have given him authority over all people, to give eternal life to all whom you have given him. ³And this is eternal life, that they may know you, the only true God, and Jesus Christ whom you have sent. ⁴I glorified you on earth by finishing the work that you gave me to do. ⁵So now, Father, glorify me in your own presence with the glory that I had in your presence before the world existed.

⁶'I have made your name known to those whom you gave me from the world. They were yours, and you gave them to me, and they have kept your word. ⁷Now they know that everything you have given me is from you; ⁸for the words that you gave to me I have given to them, and they have received them and know in truth that I came from you; and they have believed that you sent me. ⁹I am asking on their behalf; I am not asking on behalf of the world, but on behalf of those whom you gave me, because they are yours. ¹⁰All mine are yours, and yours are mine; and I have been glorified in them.

¹¹And now I am no longer in the world, but they are in the world, and I am coming to you. Holy Father, protect them in your name that you have given me, so that they may be one, as we are one. ¹²While I was with them, I protected them in your name that you have given me. I guarded them, and not one of them was lost except the one destined to be lost, so that the scripture might be fulfilled. ¹³But now I am coming to you, and I speak these things in the world so that they may have my joy made complete in themselves. ¹⁴I have given them your word, and the world has hated them because they do not belong to the world, just as I do not belong to the world. ¹⁵I am not asking you to take them out of the world, but I ask you to protect them from the evil one. ¹⁶They do not belong to the world, just as I do not belong to the world.

¹⁷Sanctify them in the truth; your word is truth. ¹⁸As you have sent me into the world, so I have sent them into the world. ¹⁹And for their sakes I sanctify myself, so that they also may be sanctified in truth.

²⁰'I ask not only on behalf of these, but also on behalf of those who will believe in me through their word, ²¹that they may all be one. As you, Father, are in me and I am in you, may they also be in us, so that the world may believe that you have sent me. ²²The glory that you have given me I have given them, so that they may be one, as we are one, ²³I in them and you in me, that they may become completely one, so that the world may know that you have sent me and have loved them even as you have loved me.

²⁴Father, I desire that those also, whom you have given me, may be with me where I am, to see my glory, which you have given me because you loved me before the foundation of the world. ²⁵'Righteous Father, the world does not know you, but I know you; and these know that you have sent me. ²⁶I made your name known to them, and I will make it known, so that the love with which you have loved me may be in them, and I in them.'

chapter EIGHTEEN

The **Betrayal** and **Arrest** of **Jesus**

After Jesus had spoken these words, he went out with his disciples across the Kidron valley to a place where there was a garden, which he and his disciples entered. ²Now Judas, who betrayed him, also knew the place, because Jesus often met there with his disciples. ³So Judas brought a detachment of soldiers together with police from the chief priests and the Pharisees, and they came there with lanterns and torches and weapons. ⁴Then Jesus, knowing all that was to happen to him, came forward and asked them,

'Whom are you looking for?' [5]They answered, 'Jesus of Nazareth.' Jesus replied, 'I am he.' Judas, who betrayed him, was standing with them. [6]When Jesus said to them, 'I am he,' they stepped back and fell to the ground. [7]Again he asked them, 'Whom are you looking for?' And they said, 'Jesus of Nazareth.' [8]Jesus answered, 'I told you that I am he. So if you are looking for me, let these men go.' [9]This was to fulfil the word that he had spoken, 'I did not lose a single one of those whom you gave me.' [10]Then Simon Peter, who had a sword, drew it, struck the high priest's slave, and cut off his right ear. The slave's name was Malchus. [11]Jesus said to Peter, 'Put your sword back into its sheath. Am I not to drink the cup that the Father has given me?'

Jesus before the High Priest

[12]So the soldiers, their officer, and the Jewish police arrested Jesus and bound him. [13]First they took him to Annas, who was the father-in-law of Caiaphas, the high priest that year. [14]Caiaphas was the one who had advised the Jews that it was better to have one person die for the people.

Peter Denies Jesus

[15]Simon Peter and another disciple followed Jesus. Since that disciple was known to the high priest, he went with Jesus into the courtyard of the high priest, [16]but Peter was standing outside at the gate. So the other disciple, who was known to the high priest, went out, spoke to the woman who guarded the gate, and brought Peter in. [17]The woman said to Peter, 'You are not also one of this man's disciples, are you?' He said, 'I am not.' [18]Now the slaves and the police had made a charcoal fire because it was cold, and they were standing around it and warming themselves. Peter also was standing with them and warming himself.

The **High Priest Questions Jesus**

[19]Then the high priest questioned Jesus about his disciples and about his teaching. [20]Jesus answered, 'I have spoken openly to the world; I have always taught in synagogues and in the temple, where all the Jews come together. I have said nothing in secret. [21]Why do you ask me? Ask those who heard what I said to them; they know what I said.' [22]When he had said this, one of the police standing nearby struck Jesus on the face, saying, 'Is that how you answer the high priest?' [23]Jesus answered, 'If I have spoken wrongly, testify to the wrong. But if I have spoken rightly, why do you strike me?' [24]Then Annas sent him bound to Caiaphas the high priest.

Peter **Denies Jesus Again**

[25]Now Simon Peter was standing and warming himself. They asked him, 'You are not also one of his disciples, are you?' He denied it and said, 'I am not.' [26]One of the slaves of the high priest, a relative of the man whose ear Peter had cut off, asked, 'Did I not see you in the garden with him?' [27]Again Peter denied it, and at that moment the cock crowed.

Jesus before Pilate

[28] Then they took Jesus from Caiaphas to Pilate's headquarters. It was early in the morning. They themselves did not enter the headquarters, so as to avoid ritual defilement and to be able to eat the Passover. [29]So Pilate went out to them and

said, 'What accusation do you bring against this man?' 30They answered, 'If this man were not a criminal, we would not have handed him over to you.' 31Pilate said to them, 'Take him yourselves and judge him according to your law.' The Jews replied, 'We are not permitted to put anyone to death.' 32(This was to fulfil what Jesus had said when he indicated the kind of death he was to die.) 33 Then Pilate entered the headquarters again, summoned Jesus, and asked him, 'Are you the King of the Jews?' 34Jesus answered, 'Do you ask this on your own, or did others tell you about me?' 35Pilate replied, 'I am not a Jew, am I? Your own nation and the chief priests have handed you over to me. What have you done?' 36Jesus answered, 'My kingdom is not from this world. If my kingdom were from this world, my followers would be fighting to keep me from being handed over to the Jews. But as it is, my kingdom is not from here.' 37Pilate asked him, 'So you are a king?' Jesus answered, 'You say that I am a king. For this I was born, and for this I came into the world, to testify to the truth. Everyone who belongs to the truth listens to my voice.' 38Pilate asked him, 'What is truth?'

Jesus Sentenced to Death

After he had said this, he went out to the Jews again and told them, 'I find no case against him. 39But you have a custom that I release someone for you at the Passover. Do you want me to release for you the King of the Jews?' 40They shouted in reply, 'Not this man, but Barabbas!' Now Barabbas was a bandit.

chapter NINETEEN

Then Pilate took Jesus and had him flogged. 2And the soldiers wove a crown of thorns and put it on his head, and they dressed him in a purple robe. 3They kept coming up to him, saying, 'Hail, King of the Jews!' and striking him on the face. 4Pilate went out again and said to them, 'Look, I am bringing him out to you to let you know that I find no case against him.' 5So Jesus came out, wearing the crown of thorns and the purple robe. Pilate said to them, 'Here is the man!' 6When the chief priests and the police saw him, they shouted, 'Crucify him! Crucify him!' Pilate said to them, 'Take him yourselves and crucify him; I find no case against him.' 7The Jews answered him, 'We have a law, and according to that law he ought to die because he has claimed to be the Son of God.' 8Now when Pilate heard this, he was more afraid than ever. 9He entered his headquarters again and asked Jesus, 'Where are you from?' But Jesus gave him no answer. 10Pilate therefore said to him, 'Do you refuse to speak to me? Do you not know that I have power to release you, and power to crucify you?' 11Jesus answered him, 'You would have no power over me unless it had been given you from above; therefore the one who handed me over to you is guilty of a greater sin.' 12From then on Pilate tried to release him, but the Jews cried out, 'If you release this man, you are no friend of the emperor. Everyone who claims to be a king sets himself against the emperor.' [13]When Pilate heard these words, he brought Jesus outside and sat on the judge's bench at a place called The Stone Pavement, or in Hebrew Gabbatha. [14]Now it was the day of Preparation for the Passover; and it was about noon. He said to the Jews, 'Here is your King!' [15]They cried out, 'Away with him! Away with him! Crucify him!' Pilate asked them, 'Shall I crucify your King?' The chief priests answered, 'We have no king but the emperor.' [16]Then he handed him over to them to be crucified.

The **Crucifixion** of **Jesus**

So they took Jesus; [17]and carrying the cross by himself, he went out to what is called The Place of the Skull, which in Hebrew is called Golgotha. [18]There they crucified him, and with him two others, one on either side, with Jesus between them.

[19]Pilate also had an inscription written and put on the cross. It read, 'Jesus of Nazareth, the King of the Jews.' [20]Many of the Jews read this inscription, because the place where Jesus was crucified was near the city; and it was written in Hebrew, in Latin, and in Greek. [21]Then the chief priests of the Jews said to Pilate, 'Do not write, "The King of the Jews," but, "This man said, I am King of the Jews."' [22]Pilate answered, 'What I have written I have written.' [23]When the soldiers had crucified Jesus, they took his clothes and divided them into four parts, one for each soldier. They also took his tunic; now the tunic was seamless, woven in one piece from the top. [24]So they said to one another, 'Let us not tear it, but cast lots for it to see who will get it.' This was to fulfil what the scripture says, 'They divided my clothes among themselves, and for my clothing they cast lots.' [25]And that

is what the soldiers did. Meanwhile, standing near the cross of Jesus were his mother, and his mother's sister, Mary the wife of Clopas, and Mary Magdalene. [26]When Jesus saw his mother and the disciple whom he loved standing beside her, he said to his mother, 'Woman, here is your son.' [27]Then he said to the disciple, 'Here is your mother.' And from that hour the disciple took her into his own home. [28]After this, when Jesus knew that all was now finished, he said (in order to fulfil the scripture), 'I am thirsty.' [29]A jar full of sour wine was standing there. So they put a sponge full of the wine on a branch of hyssop and held it to his mouth. [30]When Jesus had received the wine, he said, 'It is finished.' Then he bowed his head and gave up his spirit.

Jesus' Side Is Pierced

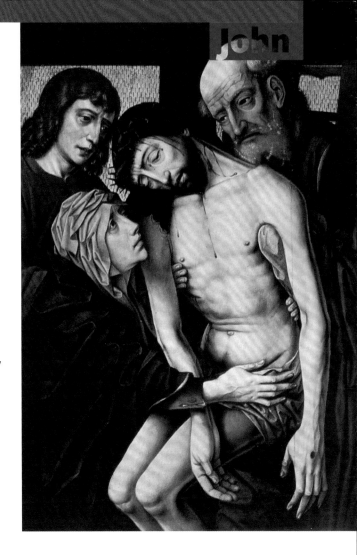

31Since it was the day of Preparation, the Jews did not want the bodies left on the cross during the sabbath, especially because that sabbath was a day of great solemnity. So they asked Pilate to have the legs of the crucified men broken and the bodies removed. 32Then the soldiers came and broke the legs of the first and of the other who had been crucified with him. 33But when they came to Jesus and saw that he was already dead, they did not break his legs. 34Instead, one of the soldiers pierced his side with a spear, and at once blood and water came out. 35(He who saw this has testified so that you also may believe. His testimony is true, and he knows that he tells the truth.) 36These things occurred so that the scripture might be fulfilled, 'None of his bones shall be broken.' 37And again another passage of scripture says, 'They will look on the one whom they have pierced.'

The Burial of Jesus

38After these things, Joseph of Arimathea, who was a disciple of Jesus, though a secret one because of his fear of the Jews, asked Pilate to let him take away the body of Jesus. Pilate gave him permission; so he came and removed his body. 39Nicodemus, who had at first come to Jesus by night, also came, bringing a mixture of myrrh and aloes, weighing about a hundred pounds. 40They took the body of Jesus and wrapped it with the spices in linen cloths, according to the burial custom of the Jews. 41Now there was a garden in the place where he was crucified, and in the garden there was a new tomb in which no one had ever been laid. 42And so, because it was the Jewish day of Preparation, and the tomb was nearby, they laid Jesus there.

chapter TWENTY

The **Resurrection** of **Jesus**

Early on the first day of the week, while it was still dark, Mary Magdalene came to the tomb and saw that the stone had been removed from the tomb. ²So she ran and went to Simon Peter and the other disciple, the one whom Jesus loved, and said to them, 'They have taken the Lord out of the tomb, and we do not know where they have laid him.' ³Then Peter and the other disciple set out and went toward the tomb. ⁴The two were running together, but the other disciple outran Peter and reached the tomb first. ⁵He bent down to look in and saw the linen wrappings lying there, but he did not go in. ⁶Then Simon Peter came, following him, and went into the tomb. He saw the linen wrappings lying there, ⁷and the cloth that had been on Jesus' head, not lying with the linen wrappings but rolled up in a place by itself. ⁸Then the other disciple, who reached the tomb first, also went in, and he saw and believed; ⁹for as yet they did not understand the scripture, that he must rise from the dead. ¹⁰Then the disciples returned to their homes.

Jesus Appears to **Mary Magdalene**

¹¹But Mary stood weeping outside the tomb. As she wept, she bent over to look into the tomb; ¹²and she saw two angels in white, sitting where the body of Jesus had been lying, one at the head and the other at the feet. ¹³They said to her, 'Woman, why are you weeping?' She said to them, 'They have taken away my Lord, and I do not know where they have laid him.' ¹⁴When she had said this, she turned around and saw Jesus standing there, but she did not know that it was Jesus. ¹⁵Jesus said to her, 'Woman, why are you

weeping? Whom are you looking for?' Supposing him to be the gardener, she said to him, 'Sir, if you have carried him away, tell me where you have laid him, and I will take him away.' [16]Jesus said to her, 'Mary!' She turned and said to him in Hebrew, 'Rabbouni!' (which means Teacher). [17]Jesus said to her, 'Do not hold on to me, because I have not yet ascended to the Father. But go to my brothers and say to them, "I am ascending to my Father and your Father, to my God and your God."' [18]Mary Magdalene went and announced to the disciples, 'I have seen the Lord'; and she told them that he had said these things to her.

Jesus Appears to the Disciples

[19]When it was evening on that day, the first day of the week, and the doors of the house where the disciples had met were locked for fear of the Jews, Jesus came and stood among them and said, 'Peace be with you.' [20]After he said this, he showed them his hands and his side. Then the disciples rejoiced when they saw the Lord. [21]Jesus said to them again, 'Peace be with you. As the Father has sent me, so I send you.' [22]When he had said this, he breathed on them and said to them, 'Receive the Holy Spirit. [23]If you forgive the sins of any, they are forgiven them; if you retain the sins of any, they are retained.'

Jesus and Thomas

[24]But Thomas (who was called the Twin), one of the twelve, was not with them when Jesus came. [25]So the other disciples told him, 'We have seen the Lord.' But he said to them, 'Unless I see the mark of the nails in his hands, and put my finger in the mark of the nails and my hand in his side, I will not believe.'
[26]A week later his disciples were again in the house, and Thomas was with them. Although the doors were shut, Jesus came and stood among them and said, 'Peace be with you.' [27]Then he said to Thomas, 'Put your finger here and see my hands. Reach out your hand and put it in my side. Do not doubt but believe.' [28]Thomas answered him, 'My Lord and my God!' [29]Jesus said to him, 'Have you believed because you have seen me? Blessed are those who have not seen and yet have come to believe.'

The **Purpose** of **This Book**

[30]Now Jesus did many other signs in the presence of his disciples, which are not written in this book. [31]But these are written so that you may come to believe that Jesus is the Messiah, the Son of God, and that through believing you may have life in his name.

chapter TWENTY-ONE

Jesus Appears to Seven Disciples

After these things Jesus showed himself again to the disciples by the Sea of Tiberias; and he showed himself in this way. ²Gathered there together were Simon Peter, Thomas called the Twin, Nathanael of Cana in Galilee, the sons of Zebedee, and two others of his disciples. ³Simon Peter said to them, 'I am going fishing.' They said to him, 'We will go with you.' They went out and got into the boat, but that night they caught nothing. ⁴Just after daybreak, Jesus stood on the beach; but the disciples did not know that it was Jesus. ⁵Jesus said to them, 'Children, you have no fish, have you?' They answered him, 'No.' ⁶He said to them, 'Cast the net to the right side of the boat, and you will find some.' So they cast it, and now they were not able to haul it in because

there were so many fish. ⁷That disciple whom Jesus loved said to Peter, 'It is the Lord!' When Simon Peter heard that it was the Lord, he put on some clothes, for he was naked, and jumped into the sea. ⁸But the other disciples came in the boat, dragging the net full of fish, for they were not far from the land, only about a hundred yards off. ⁹When they had gone ashore, they saw a charcoal fire there, with fish on it, and bread. ¹⁰Jesus said to them, 'Bring some of the fish that you have just caught.' ¹¹So Simon Peter went aboard and hauled the net ashore, full of large fish, a hundred fifty-three of them; and though there were so many, the net was not torn. ¹²Jesus said to them, 'Come and have breakfast.' Now none of the disciples dared to ask him, 'Who are you?' because they knew it was the Lord. ¹³Jesus came and took the bread and gave it to them, and did the same with the fish. ¹⁴This was now the third time that Jesus appeared to the disciples after he was raised from the dead.

Jesus and Peter

[15]When they had finished breakfast, Jesus said to Simon Peter, 'Simon son of John, do you love me more than these?' He said to him, 'Yes, Lord; you know that I love you.' Jesus said to him, 'Feed my lambs.' [16]A second time he said to him, 'Simon son of John, do you love me?' He said to him, 'Yes, Lord; you know that I love you.' Jesus said to him, 'Tend my sheep.' [17]He said to him the third time, 'Simon son of John, do you love me?' Peter felt hurt because he said to him the third time, 'Do you love me?' And he said to him, 'Lord, you know everything; you know that I love you.' Jesus said to him, 'Feed my sheep. [18]Very truly, I tell you, when you were younger, you used to fasten your own belt and to go wherever you wished. But when you grow old, you will stretch out your hands, and someone else will fasten a belt around you and take you where you do not wish to go.' [19](He said this to indicate the kind of death by which he would glorify God.) After this he said to him, 'Follow me.'

Jesus and the Beloved Disciple

[20] Peter turned and saw the disciple whom Jesus loved following them; he was the one who had reclined next to Jesus at the supper and had said, 'Lord, who is it that is going to betray you?' [21]When Peter saw him, he said to Jesus, 'Lord, what about him?' [22]Jesus said to him, 'If it is my will that he remain until I come, what is that to you? Follow me!' [23]So the rumour spread in the community that this disciple would not die. Yet Jesus did not say to him that he would not die, but, 'If it is my will that he remain until I come, what is that to you?'

A SHORT EPILOGUE REFERRING TO THE GREAT MASS OF THE SAVIOUR'S WORDS AND WORKS NOT RECORDED IN THE GOSPEL (21:24-25)

[24]This is the disciple who is testifying to these things and has written them, and we know that his testimony is true. [25]But there are also many other things that Jesus did; if every one of them were written down, I suppose that the world itself could not contain the books that would be written.

Lectio divina

Lectio divina (meaning 'divine reading' or 'holy reading') is an ancient method of paying attention to God's Word in Scripture in order to achieve a fuller understanding of the message and thus be better able to take it to heart in daily life. It was first practiced in the early Christian monasteries. Pope Benedict XVI said: 'I would like in particular to recall and recommend the ancient tradition of *lectio divina*: the diligent reading of Sacred Scripture accompanied by prayer brings about that intimate dialogue in which the person reading hears God who is speaking, and, in praying, responds with trusting openness of heart.'

Lectio divina is a particularly simple approach to prayer. It can be used individually or in groups. Ideally, you should choose the same time each day for this exercise and in a place free of distraction so that a daily habit will be learned.

So, choose a text of Scripture, something fairly brief and engaging. Then:

Lectio (read): Slowly read the text, being alert for God's Word to your life; notice what stands out for you or seems significant.

Meditatio (meditate): Read the text again. Pause and talk to God about what you are hearing. Meditation is like talking to God.

Contemplatio (contemplate): Read again. Now listen to and receive what God may be saying to you. Contemplation is like listening to God.

Oratio (pray): Recognise and pray whatever may be the deep desire of your heart.

Then some traditions add:

Actio (action): What does this study and prayer time call you to do? How will you take it to heart in your life now?

People from all walks of life are realising the benefits of this type of spiritual exercise. *Lectio divina* allows you to explore the deep wisdom of Scripture and to experience God in a very personal way.

Index